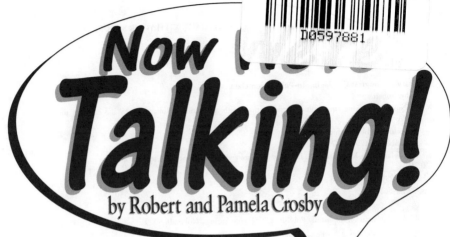

Now We're Talking!

by Robert and Pamela Crosby

Questions to Build Intimacy with Your Spouse

FOCUS ON THE FAMILY

PUBLISHING

Colorado Springs, Colorado

NOW WE'RE TALKING! QUESTIONS TO BUILD INTIMACY WITH YOUR SPOUSE

Copyright © 1996 by Robert C. Crosby and Pamela Crosby
All rights reserved. International copyright secured.

Library of Congress Cataloging-in-Publication Data
Crosby, Robert
    Now we're talking : questions to build intimacy with your spouse / Robert Crosby and Pamela Crosby.
        p. c.m.
    Includes bibliographical references.
    ISBN 1-56179-473-2
        1. Marriage—Miscellanea. 2. Intimacy (Psychology)—Miscellanea. I. Crosby, Pamela.
II. Title.
HQ734.C8956   1996
306.81—dc20
                                                    96-21530
                                                        CIP

Published by Focus on the Family Publishing, Colorado Springs, Colorado 80995.

Distributed in the U.S.A. and Canada by Word Books, Dallas, Texas.

Unless otherwise indicated, Scripture taken from the HOLY BIBLE, NEW INTERNATIONAL VERSION ® , (NIV) ® .
Copyright © 1973, 1978, 1984 by International Bible Society. Used by permission of Zondervan Publishing House. All
rights reserved.

No part of this publication may be reproduced, stored in a retrieval system, or transmitted in any form or by any means—
electronic, mechanical, photocopy, recording, or otherwise—without prior permission of the publisher.

Focus on the Family books are available at special quantity discounts when purchased in bulk by corporations, organiza-
tions, churches, or groups. Special imprints, messages, and excerpts can be produced to meet your needs. For more infor-
mation, contact: Sales Dept., Focus on the Family Publishing, 8605 Explorer Dr., Colorado Springs, CO 80920; or phone
(719) 531-3400.

Editor: Colorado Wordmaster
Cover Designer: Candi L. Park

Printed in the United States of America

96 97 98 99 00 01 02 03/10 9 8 7 6 5 4 3 2 1

To

Mr. & Mrs.
Robert C. Crosby Jr.

&

The Rev. & Mrs.
David H. Krist

For giving us homes full of love,

full of wonderful conversation,

full of life.

CONTENTS

Introduction

IT ALL BEGAN
WITH A QUESTION

Strolling down the sidewalk from our college cafeteria to the dormitories, I (Bob) was enjoying a casual conversation with this young lady who, unbeknownst to me, was about to pop a question.

Pam was a friend of one of my friends, and over the previous couple of weeks, had become my friend as well. I enjoyed talking to her, but, in my mind at least, this relationship didn't have dating potential. At that time, I was trying to date another girl—and Pam knew it.

"Robert, would you go with me to the Sadie Hawkins party?"

For the first time in my life, *I* was being asked out. My initial reaction was that it felt really great. I found Pam's question irresistible.

"Sure, I'd love to go with you!"

The rest is history. We fell in "like," then in love. Ten months later, I asked another important question, and she said, "Yes!" Love, marriage, and baby carriages (four of them) have followed. And to think it all began with a question. This thing called question-asking can be downright life-changing, can't it?

Jesus Christ knew that and, as a result, used questions with amazing frequency.

"Who do people say that I am?"

"Who do you say that I am?"

"What will it profit a man if he gains the whole world and loses his own soul?"

"Where is your faith?"

Another great question emerges in my mind: If question-asking is so central to dating, how important is it to developing and cultivating a marriage?

Very.

Dale Carnegie once put it this way: "You'll gain more friends in three minutes by getting interested in other people than you will in three months of trying to get them interested in you." In a similar vein, you'll cultivate more intimacy in your marriage relationship in three minutes of thoughtful and considerate question-asking than you will in three months of trying to impress your spouse.

This book is designed to help husbands and wives ask each other great questions. We hope that it serves as "lighter fluid" for the romantic fire.

The first part of the book is about the benefits and techniques of putting questions to work more fully in your marriage relationship. The second part provides dozens and dozens of questions you can use to cultivate intimacy with your husband or wife.

You may wish to read this book together with your spouse, covering a chapter a week and then asking each other some questions from Part Two. You may choose to read it on your own and then use at least one question each day at an appropriate moment. Your choice may be to keep the book in your car glove compartment and grab a great question or two just before you walk into the house after work. Eventually, you will find yourself formulating your own great questions.

So many people's influences are woven through these pages. To name a few, we are grateful to Brad Lewis at *Christian Parenting Today* for nurturing an idea. What an encouragement we have received from the enthusiasm Dean Merrill and Al Janssen have shown over this project. Thanks for sharing the vision.

Our hope and prayer are that somehow this tool will assist you in cultivating quality time with your spouse and opening your soul a bit more. Remember, there is more to know about that person you married than you have yet discovered.

Part One

ASKING GREAT QUESTIONS

*For this reason a man will leave his father and mother and be
united to his wife, and the two will become one flesh.*

Ephesians 5:31

Chapter One

WHAT WE DON'T KNOW CAN INDEED HURT US

The one thing most men lack is the one thing most women want: Intimacy.

Patrick Morley[1]

Men ask questions all the time . . . at work and at play. A junior executive taps a senior associate for advice that will help him succeed. A first-year auto body repair apprentice asks a master of the trade why he does what he does to achieve a smooth surface. What motivates them both is the anticipation of a better grade, a broader understanding, a promotion, a better reputation, or greater respect.

Women ask questions frequently as well . . . in the business world, in the neighborhood, in phone calls to family members, and at church. The topics can range from corporate policy to domestic insights to how to encourage a child's learning.

But what about asking questions of your spouse? What will that really accomplish?

Questions are invitations. They welcome people, invite people in. They encourage individuals to confide in us, to unload, to dream, to dare, and to share. They break through the stony surfaces that keep us from growing close.

Many wives and husbands today are starving for more

intimacy in their lives. Consider this telling letter from a
lonely lady, sent to a pastor:

> The kids are in bed. There's nothing on TV
> tonight. I ask my husband if he minds if I
> turn the tube off. He grunts.
>
> As I walk to the set, my mind is racing.
> Maybe, just maybe, tonight we'll talk. I mean,
> we'll have a conversation that consists of more
> than my usual questions and his mumbled
> one-word answers . . . or no answer at all.
>
> Silence—I live in a world of continuous
> noise, but between him and myself, silence.
> Please—O God, let him open up. I initiate
> (once again, for the thousandth time). My heart
> pounds—oh, how can I word it this time?
> What can I say that will open the door just to
> talk? I don't have to have a deep, meaningful
> conversation. Just something!

As I open my mouth—he gets up and goes to the bedroom. The door closes behind him. The crack of light showing under the door gives way to darkness. So does my hope.

I sit alone on the couch. My heart begins to ache. I'm tired of being alone. Hey, I'm married! I have been for years. Why do I sit alone?[2]

Rod Cooper, a Promise Keeper leader, pronounces *intimacy* as "into-me-see!" That's good. It says much about what intimacy brings and calls for. It also describes exactly what effective questions should draw upon. Undoubtedly, the man who chooses to give his wife genuine intimacy gives her much more than a marriage license. He gives her himself . . . unmasked, uncovered, and unlimited.

Intimacy cannot be forced out, driven out, or demanded. No remote control exists that, upon command, can summon the thoughts, concerns, feelings, and longings of a spouse's soul. Intimacy is something that must be drawn out in a relationship. Proverbs 20:5 says, "The purposes of a man's heart are deep waters, but a man of understanding *draws* them out" (emphasis added).

Intimacy means that I know who you are at the deepest level, and I accept you.

Intimacy is reaching out to understand each other in the face of busy schedules, different personalities, embarrassing secrets, and past hurts.

Intimacy is a block of time given freely or sacrificially to the one to whom you have made vows.

Intimacy in marriage is "an unhindered emotional closeness in our inmost being through which husband and wife are continually sensitive and responsive to one another."[3]

Intimacy is opening up to your mate when he/she reaches out.

Intimacy is being spiritually, intellectually, and emotionally familiar with the deepest nature of your partner's mind, soul, body, and spirit.

Intimacy is the fusion of two distinct lives headed in

two distinct directions into a single journey of one flesh.[4]

There is so much that we *can* and *need* to be asked about. One of the best ways to discover the most effective questions to ask your spouse is to open your own eyes and first ask yourself a few, such as:

Look Around

What are the most difficult situations we're facing as a couple?

Which part of my spouse's week or day does he/she most look forward to?

What responsibilities is he/she facing that are currently the most challenging?

How much support does he/she feel from me at home?

What are his/her greatest felt needs today?

Look Within

What kinds of questions is he/she seeking answers for?

Who is the most difficult person he/she has to deal with?

What areas of uncertainty or insecurity does he/she struggle with most?

In what parts of life does he/she feel the most fulfilled?

Look Up

Has he/she realized most of his/her dreams in life? Any of them?

What accomplishments is he/she proudest of?

How could I help one of his/her dreams come true?

Where would he/she really like to go on vacation this year?

Look Closer

Are we sharing our deepest fears and highest hopes with each other? What are they?

What are the most encouraging words I have offered him/her recently?

When do we feel closest to each other?

Am I being honest with him/her about all the areas of my life?

Our own innate selfishness tends to work daily against sensitivity to one another in marriage. As a result, wise spouses take determined steps to lay aside their own concerns and consider the current needs of the other.

"You should never stop chasing the person you marry," says one pastor-friend, Ron Domina. As a matter of fact, the Bible says it this way: "Therefore shall a man leave his father and his mother, and shall cleave unto his wife: and they shall be one flesh" (Gen. 2:24, KJV). The Hebrew word for "cleave" is *dabaq,* which literally means to "follow close" or to "pursue hard." Too often after the knot is tied, the life in a relationship begins to die because a man and a woman stop *pursuing* one another. They no longer endeavor to get closer relationally or emotionally.

Intimacy flourishes when a man and a woman refuse to end the adventure of asking great questions, listening closely, and sharing deeply. The benefits of doing so are not to be missed.

Notes

1. Patrick M. Morley, *Two-Part Harmony* (Nashville: Thomas Nelson, 1994), p. 78.

2. Patrick M. Morley, *The Seven Seasons of a Man's Life* (Nashville: Thomas Nelson, 1995), pp. 68–69.

3. Gloria Okes Perkins, "Intimacy: A Realistic Approach," *Discipleship Journal* 54 (1989): 44.

4. Morley, *Two-Part Harmony,* pp. 78–79.

Chapter Two

TEN BENEFITS
OF ASKING
GREAT QUESTIONS

Although question-asking can, at times, produce tension or stir up difficult emotions in a relationship, the benefits far outweigh the problems. Here are 10 ways questions can strengthen and enhance your marriage:

1. Questions let your spouse know you're genuinely interested in his/her feelings and opinions. The husband who chooses to treasure the soul of his spouse not only strengthens his wife but also his marriage and, ultimately, himself. By the same token, when a wife reveres and respects her husband's insights and opinions, it strengthens his sense of significance.

2. Questions invite your spouse to confide in you, to open his/her life to you more fully. All too often when a wife says, "Can we talk?" a husband hears her saying, *I have some things I want to complain about!* or *I want to give you some advice!* More often, however, the wife is saying on a deeper level, *I really need someone to confide in.*

I need someone who will listen and patiently help me gain a sense of perspective and wisdom. Can I safely be sincere with you? Will you be that man for me?

Perhaps, in a real sense, the essence of marriage occurs when a spouse compassionately, carefully opens a mate's soul.

3. Questions lead to a more accurate view of the family's real needs. Insecure men and women generally shy away from questions. The mate who bravely chooses to tap a spouse's soul will undoubtedly be confronted, at times, with hard truth. Ultimately, the only way a man or woman can accurately diagnose a family's greatest needs is to take a hard look at the gaping holes, the hardened soil, and the untapped potential that exist within that family. Then and only then can he or she begin, with God's help, to repair, to restore, to confront, and to build.

4. Questions adjust your expectations of your spouse. Unrealistic idealism works furiously against intimacy. On the other hand, grace cultivates it. Perhaps one way to define grace is "realistic acceptance." Great questions help us to discover what is true about our spouses, not just what we *want* to be true.

5. Questions open the door for your spouse to verbalize concerns, unload worries, and relieve stress. Wise and blessed is the spouse who provides a marriage partner with a safe place, a refuge, in which to express some of the struggles that have built up each day.

6. Questions give a spouse an invitation to express honestly without feeling like a nag. It takes a stouthearted man to willingly invite the concerns and critiques of his wife. And yet, the right question can validate a wife's strongly felt opinions and create an atmosphere in which she can safely express them.

7. Questions draw upon a spouse's dreams, longings, and desires, creating a clear agenda for ongoing encouragement. Many men wonder, "How can I encourage my wife? What can I do to lift her spirits?" Many wives wonder, "How can I build my husband's confidence? What kind of support does he most need from me?" The best answer we know is to *stop wondering* and *just ask.*

8. Questions assist greatly in getting to know the soul of the person you married, the real person inside. If indeed "these two shall become one," as the Bible says, it is God's intention that husbands and wives initiate this process again and again in deeper and more meaningful ways.

9. Questions do more, over the long haul, than merely draw upon opinions; they draw upon God-given talents, spiritual gifts, and abilities. The spouse in your life is not only your spouse; he/she is an *individual.* The person who overlooks or suppresses this aspect will end up with diminished intimacy, feelings of resentment, and, in many cases, the shipwreck of what was once a wonderful marriage.

10. Questions inspire more questions! Get ready—this intimacy thing is a two-way street. Don't attempt to ask your husband/wife great questions unless you are willing to answer a few yourself.

And without asking questions in a relationship, there is no depth.

Chapter Three

TURNING
GOOD QUESTIONS
INTO GREAT ONES

"What do you want to do tonight?"

"Honey, you're the one asking me out. Don't you have any plans or ideas?"

"It doesn't really matter to me. Whatever you want to do will be fine."

Ever had a conversation like that with your spouse? When a question is vague, dull, unrefined, or off the top of the head, the response usually falls far short of what was hoped for.

In contrast, how does this interchange strike you?

"What is the most fun we've ever had on a date?"

"Oh, the time we rode our bikes and you took me to that little bagel shop for lunch together."

"Well then, how would you like to do that again today?"

(The resulting smile on her face says it all!)

Ultimately, great questions come down to three key components: texture, technique, and timing.

THE TEXTURE OF A GREAT QUESTION

1. Get beyond "yes" and "no." Nothing spoils a conversation more than asking questions that can be answered with one word. Such questions merely search out facts; they fail to engage the personality, mind, or opinions of another.

2. Go for specifics. For example, which of the following makes you more eager to respond?

"So, how was your day?"

or

"Which part of your day did you enjoy the most? Which part of your day was the most difficult?"

3. Why ask why? We tend to ask "why" questions much too early in a conversation. Like a submarine suddenly diving to the ocean floor without adjusting the cabin pressure, "why" questions can go for too much too quickly. They storm into places where angels fear to tread, without considering whether the person is ready.

Remember, when you seek to get to the heart of issues facing you and your spouse, you are dealing with a fragile human soul. The "why" approach says, "Why are you so tense tonight? Why are you taking your anger out on me?" A better way is to say, "You seem to have a lot on your mind. Would you mind if we sit down and have a cup of coffee together? Would you be willing to take time today?"

Or, "How is your emotional bank doing today? Overdrawn? Full? Running low? How can you tell?"

Or, "What kinds of things have contributed to how you're feeling right now?"

4. Check the fuel first. Before asking your spouse a question, ask yourself: *What is motivating me to ask this question right now? Curiosity? Anger? Interest? Suspicion? Hope? Concern? Frustration?*

Consider the scripture that says, "A word aptly spoken is like apples of gold in settings of silver" (Prov. 25:11).

The word *aptly* implies not only the right words and the right timing, but also the right tone.

The words ("apples of gold") are important, but so is the place and manner in which we ask ("settings of silver"). One "setting of silver" for Pam to receive a question would be a room of peace, with no noisy children and no one calling "Mom" or "Dad" every few minutes. The effective communicator in a marriage is careful to monitor the timing, the texture, *and* the tone.

THE TECHNIQUE AND TIMING OF A GREAT QUESTION

1. Wade before you dive. Respectfully and carefully consider the levels of your spouse's openness and vulnerability. The most effective question-asking begins in the *shallow* end of the pool, then gradually goes *deeper.*

The following list represents 10 levels of intimate question-asking that a man and a woman can journey through as they seek to grow closer and to know one another. You'll notice that all the questions in Part Two of this book have been arranged accordingly. These are the steps we have found helpful to keep in mind as we approach each other in conversation, ranging from more shallow items to deeper ones:

1. Favorites—things a person most enjoys

2. Fun—recreation, entertainment, and activities a person looks forward to

3. Fond Memories—the experiences in life one treasures most

4. Family—the people who make up one's sense of "home"

5. Friends—the people we feel closest to in life

6. Feelings—the emotions we carry in our lives and within our souls

7. Finances—the resource responsibilities in our lives

8. Failures and Fears—our weaknesses, disappointments, and shortcomings

9. The Future—the dreams, hopes, and aspirations for our tomorrows

10. Faith—what we believe about God, ourselves, and the world we live in

2. Avoid leading questions. Great questions are invitations, not cattle prods. It is easy to fall into the trap of using questions to compel people to come to *our* conclusions, instead of genuinely getting a sense of what they are thinking and feeling. Leading questions tend to take on a rapid-fire, bullet form in which the questioner is bent upon getting the spouse to see things his/her way.

The best way to avoid this is to take ample time to wholeheartedly listen to your spouse's responses. People can usually tell when they are being heard and when they are merely being humored.

3. Consider the other person's world. The best questions are those that arise when we endeavor to empathize with our spouse. Often a day in the life of a husband and wife can be poles apart emotionally and experientially. The wise man or woman takes time to consider the feelings and experiences that may have filled the other person's day.

4. Force yourself to "switch gears." As I (Bob) get ready to head home at the end of a workday, it helps me greatly to consciously lay aside the work orientation and to open up thoughts of family. I do this by asking myself what I call "wondering questions":

"I wonder how Pam's day went today?"

"I wonder what the kids will be doing when I get home?"

"I wonder how I can reconnect with my wife and kids within the first few minutes?"

"I wonder what we could do together tonight as a family?"

"I wonder what I can say to my family to let them know they're special to me?"

If you have a long commute home, you may wish to identify a landmark of some sort at which point you will "shift gears" every day. If your commute is short like mine, take an extra drive or two around the block. You, and your family, will be glad you did!

5. Don't force questions—place them politely. The best time to ask a question is not when you want to ask it, but when your spouse is ready to respond. Learning to discern the seasons of openness in your relationship is an art you will spend a lifetime perfecting.

6. Ask clarifying questions. Sometimes the first query doesn't get the job done. Learn to follow up and make sure you understand what the other person is trying to say.

7. Make use of "the pregnant pause." After you've asked a question, don't be afraid to wait. Give the question a chance to sink in. To hurriedly interject follow-up comments short-circuits the genuine responses your spouse was just getting ready to express. Ask, then wait. You may be surprised at what you discover.

Chapter Four

KNOWING HIM . . . KNOWING HER

Most marital difficulties center around one fact—men and women are TOTALLY different. The differences (emotional, mental, and physical) are so extreme that without a concentrated effort to understand them, it is nearly impossible to have a happy marriage.

Gary Smalley[1]

The sexes tend to cope with stress differently. According to one author, men go to their caves, and women talk. In an effort to overcome stresses or to feel better when facing them, women tend to *talk it out,* whereas men seek time and space to *solve their problems alone.*

That is not the only communication difference between men and women. Not long ago we came across this list on the Internet on how to interpret a spouse's comments:

When she says . . .	What she really means . . .
"We need . . ."	*I want . . .*
"It's your decision."	*The correct decision should be obvious by now!*
"Do what you want."	*You'll pay for this later!*
"Sure . . . go ahead."	*I don't want you to do that.*
"I'm not upset."	*Of course I'm upset, you jerk!*

"You're certainly attentive tonight."

Is sex all you ever think about?

"The kitchen is so inconvenient."

I want a new house.

"The trash is full."

Take it out!

"The dog is barking."

Go outside in the rain in your underwear and see what's wrong!

"I want new curtains."

. . . and carpeting, and furniture, and wallpaper . . .

"I heard a noise."

I noticed you were almost asleep.

"How much do you love me?"

I did something today you're really not going to like.

"Nothing is wrong."

Everything is wrong.

"I don't want to talk about it."

Go away! I'm still building up steam.

"I'll be ready in a minute."   *Take off your shoes and find a good football game on TV.*

"Am I fat?"   *Tell me I'm beautiful.*

"You have to learn to communicate."   *Just agree with me.*

"Are you listening?"   *Too late, you're dead. . . .*

Of course, there's a second part to this list:

When he says . . .	**What he really means . . .**
"You look nice tonight."	*I want to have sex.*
"Boy, am I hungry!"	*Make me something to eat and serve it to me on the couch.*
"It's too expensive."	*You could get a neat computer for that!*

"It's a beautiful day."	*It's too hot to do yard work.*
"I had a tough day at work today."	*YOU take out the trash!*
"I like my old suit just fine."	*I don't want to go anywhere that I have to wear a suit.*
"I have a surprise."	*I bought something really stupid.*
"Why don't you get a job?"	*You bought something really stupid.*
"Are you still awake?"	*I want to have sex again.*
"Let's go out for dinner."	*Whatever is cooking smells awful.*
"The legal system in this country is so dysfunctional."	*I got a speeding ticket.*

| "You can't mow the lawn when the grass is wet." | *There's a game on the tube.* |
| "Why don't you stop working?" | *You're always too tired to have sex.* |

Underneath the humor of those lists is a lot of truth. Men and women are indeed wired differently, and to communicate with each other takes adapting.

One of the better insights we've read comes from John Gray, author of the best-seller *Men Are from Mars, Women Are from Venus:*

> Men . . . become impatient when women talk about problems in great detail. A man mistakenly assumes that when a woman talks in great detail that all the details are necessary for him to find a solution to her problem. He struggles to find their relevance and becomes impatient. Again he doesn't realize that she is looking not for a solution from

him but for his caring and understanding.

In addition, listening is difficult for a man because he mistakenly assumes there is a logical order when she randomly changes from one problem to another. After she has shared three or four problems he becomes extremely frustrated and confused trying logically to relate these problems.

Another reason a man may resist listening is that he is looking for the bottom line. He cannot begin formulating his solution until he knows the outcome. The more details she gives the more he is frustrated while listening. His frustration is lessened if he can remember that talking in detail is helping her to feel good; then he can relax.[2]

When it comes to communicating, here are some things a woman should remember:

- When men become uncaring or distant toward a woman, it is usually because they're afraid of something.
- Men are more naturally motivated to achieve goals than to absorb moments.
- Men fear nothing more than failure.
- Men are motivated by feeling significant.
- Men want to manage their own problems (the "Mr. Fix-It!" syndrome).
- Men always want to "get to the bottom line."
- Men tend to "report" more than converse. Just listen to a man on the phone. He's brief, utilitarian, and to the point: "Okay . . . All right . . . Got it . . . Be there at 8:00 . . . See ya."

So the best way to get a preoccupied man to talk is not to overwhelm him with too many questions at once, but to cultivate conversation carefully and patiently. John Gray offers his tips to women:

When a woman wants to talk or feels the need to get close, she should do the talking and not expect a man to initiate the conversation. To initiate a conversation she needs to be the first to begin sharing, even if her partner has little to say. As she appreciates him for listening, gradually he will have more to say.

A man can be very open to having a conversation with a woman but at first have nothing to say. What women don't know about [men] is that they need to have a reason to talk. They don't talk just for the sake of sharing. But when a woman talks for a while, a man will start to open up and share how he relates to what she has shared. . . .

A woman sharing her thoughts naturally motivates a man to talk. But when he feels a demand is being made that he talk, his mind goes blank. He has nothing to say. Even if he has something to say he will resist because he feels her demand.[3]

In the next chapter, we will review perhaps the most important component of this entire book: the attitude of asking.

Notes

1. Gary Smalley, *If Only He Knew* (Grand Rapids: Zondervan, 1979), p. 13.

2. John Gray, *Men Are from Mars, Women Are from Venus* (New York: HarperCollins, 1992), pp. 38–39.

3. Ibid., p. 100.

Chapter Five

THE ATTITUDE
OF ASKING

"He doesn't ask me about myself anymore—my interests, my dreams, my desires."

"The only time he gets interested in me now is when he wants to have sex."

"He doesn't really know how I feel . . . and I don't think he wants to know."

More than one wife has felt that way.

"She is so focused on what I'm not doing at home that she never asks about what I am doing at work."

"All she ever asks me about is the current 'Honey-Do List' and when I am going to get to it!"

"We just aren't interested in the same things anymore."

Similar frustrations have fired up in more than one man's soul.

Ironically, some of the same couples who begin their relationships with three-hour phone calls and endless cards and letters find themselves one day sitting across from each other at a restaurant with nothing to say, no more questions to ask, and feeling next to nothing in common. The person who was once the focus of his/her life and dreams is now a person from whom he/she feels completely detached. At one point they never seemed to have enough time to talk; now there's not enough to talk *about*.

Asking is not just an activity; it is an attitude to develop. At its best, asking is fueled by powerful motivators—curiosity, wonder, interest, desire, intrigue, and appreciation.

What keeps us from asking? Why is it that some spouses hesitate to ask and respond to questions? Why wouldn't they want to peer into the heart and soul of the person they promised to "love and to cherish . . . till death do us part"?

In some cases, the problem stems from a childhood diet of reprimands such as:

"Would you be quiet!?"

"I don't want to hear it!"

"Shut your mouth and keep it shut!"

"You're getting on my nerves!"

"No more questions!"

"Can't you do anything but ask questions?"

"I'm busy right now!"

"Later!"

"It will just have to wait!"

"In a minute!"

"What do you want *now?*"

"If you can't say something nice, don't say anything at all."

"No comments from the peanut gallery."

"Bite your tongue!"

While some childhood behavior may have warranted correction, the sad fact is that many men and women were raised with these kinds of comments as the rule and not the exception. The general home atmosphere was nonconversant, if not verbally combative or abusive. Children were to be "seen and not heard," meals were arranged around the television set, youngsters were told *what to do* but never asked *how they felt*, and the only questions kids heard their moms and dads ask each other were ones like "Did you take the garbage out yet?" and "What's for supper?"

In this case, asking great questions and communicating openly is something that has to be learned.

Another factor that keeps many spouses from asking is the misconception "If we love each other, we shouldn't have to ask." Such a false notion was portrayed in the 1970s box-office hit *Love Story*, from which sprang the much-publicized quote "Love means never having to say you're sorry." Nothing could be further from the truth.

Great marriages necessitate great conversations. They find their genesis in strong and open communication between two people.

According to the Bible, the best way to receive is simply to ask. Whether praying to God or cultivating a relationship with your spouse, few things will open doors and connect hearts like asking.

Throughout history, more often than not the spoils have gone to those who asked. A lovely young lady's hand has gone to the one who proposed, not to the one who hesitated or shied away. The thriving new business venture has been launched by the entrepreneur who raised the right questions, found the right answers, and, as a result, took the right steps. The wandering prodigal teenager has been won not by the distant skeptic but by the caring question-asker.

The most vibrant marriages and families are those who have embraced the attitude of asking. Such souls are passionate about learning all they can about each other and about life and the world around them. They are grateful for what they have but eager to learn and discover so much more! In their minds, to live is to engage. The attitude of asking involves a passionate pursuit, an intriguing perspective, and wonderfully enriching intimacies. They are yours for the asking.

Part Two

GREAT QUESTIONS TO ASK YOUR SPOUSE

Here they are! Hundreds of questions you can put to
work right away in cultivating your marriage and
building intimacy.

They are arranged in 10 different sections or levels, beginning
with the most general and least confrontive (i.e., the "shallow end
of the pool") and moving to the more intimate and personal.

Level One

ASKING ABOUT FAVORITES

How many blankets do you really like to have on the bed?

At what temperature do you like to keep our house set?

Of all the gifts I've given you over the years, which ones have meant the most to you?

What is your favorite music to listen to at night?

Which outfits of mine do you like the most? Why those?

What is your favorite chore to do at home? Which one is your least favorite?

Which cologne/perfume do you most like for me to wear? Why that one?

What are three things we love to do together? Can we do them again soon? When?

In which room in our house do you wish we spent more time together? Why?

What was the best meal you've ever had in a restaurant? May I take you there this week?

What is your favorite time of the day? Why then?

What's the best book you've read recently? Tell me about it. What did you like about it?

What has been the brightest part of your day today?

What are your favorite kinds of flowers? Why those?

What are your favorite perfumes? What do you like about them?

F
A
V
O
R
I
T
E
S

What was the best novel you ever read? What made it so great? Tell me about it! If you were to pick the actors for a movie of this book, who would play the leads?

Who was your favorite teacher while you were growing up? What about this person impressed you the most?

What is your absolute favorite dessert to have in a restaurant? Would you like to get some right now?

If you could store up only one hour's worth of memory in your mind, which hour of our married lives would you most want to remember? Why?

Who had the most positive influence on you as a child?

What is one day you would love to live over again?

Which Bible character do you most identify with?

What famous person would you most like to meet? Why?

If you could coach any professional sports team, which one would you choose? What would you do the first week on the job?

If you could have the autograph of anyone in the world, who would you choose?

If you could own the world's largest collection of anything, what would it be?

What friends of ours do you feel the most comfortable with? To what do you attribute that?

What friends of ours do you feel the least comfortable with? How come?

F
A
V
O
R
I
T
E
S

Which popular songs were your favorites growing up?
List five. Which ones did you listen to the most?

Which holiday do you enjoy the most? Why that one?

Level Two

ASKING ABOUT FUN

If we could have two days to spend alone together, how would you like to spend them? Where would you like to go? What would you like to do?

What are some things you wish you had more time for? What can I do to help you find the time to do some of them?

What was the best date we ever had? Where did we go? What did we do?

What are you currently looking forward to? Do we plan enough "fun times" together to keep you motivated and encouraged?

What is the most spontaneous, fun thing we have ever done?

What hobby of yours do you most enjoy? Which one makes you feel the most relaxed?

Can we take some time to plan our vacation for this year well in advance? Where would you most like to go? What would you like to do?

If we could just drop what we're doing right now and go do something fun for the rest of the afternoon, what would it be? What would you most enjoy doing right now? Let's go!

F
U
N

When was the last time something exciting happened in your life? Describe it to me.

What can we do to keep our marriage fulfilling and fun?

When was the last time you and I had a really good laugh? What caused it? What effect did laughing have on you?

What is one thing you would like to try that you're convinced I would never be willing to do? Where do I sign up?!

How many ways are there to squeeze a toothpaste tube, anyway? Which of us is the most creative at it?

What in your life today brings you the greatest sense of joy and fulfillment?

What is your idea of a really relaxed evening? What would it consist of?

What is one thing you just wish you had more time for?

How would you like it if I made supper tonight?

How do you really feel about the way I sing?

If you and I went on a date together and had only $10 to spend, what would you like to do?

What is one thing I know how to do that you would like me to teach you? Shall we schedule the first lesson?

Would you like to learn how to use the computer? . . . get on the Internet?

When you play a sport, do you prefer competing against someone who is worse or better than you? What does that tell you about yourself?

If you could relive any year in your life, without changing a thing, which year would you choose?

If you could possess any extraordinary talent in one of the arts, what would you choose?

F
U
N

If you could be a contestant on any game show, which one would you select?

If you could own any professional sports team, which one would you choose?

If you could be president of the United States for one day, what's the first thing you would do?

If you could be on the cover of any magazine, which one would you pick?

Level Three

ASKING ABOUT
FOND MEMORIES

What is one of the most adventurous things you've ever done?

How many times did you move as a child? What was that experience like for you?

Did you have an imaginary friend growing up? What was its name? Did anyone else know about this?

What is your earliest memory?

Did you enjoy physical education in school as a kid? Were you the first or the last picked on gym teams?

What was your first-grade teacher like? What did you think of her/him? Do you remember her/his name?

Do you remember your first day at school? What was it like?

What are your most vivid childhood vacation memories? Where did you go? What did you do?

How would you describe your parents' marriage while you were growing up?

Did you get along well with your parents during your teen years? How about your siblings?

Did you play tricks on anyone in your family growing up? Which times do you recall?

How important were family pets in your home as a child?

Can you list all the pets you had growing up? Go ahead.

Has your family ever been superstitious? How so?

M
E
M
O
R
I
E
S

What hobbies did your parents enjoy during your childhood?

What were your parents' favorite television shows when you were a child?

What role did prayer play in your home as a child?

Do you remember any stories about what your grandparents were like as children? . . . as teenagers?

Did your family listen to much music when you were a child? What kinds?

How important were books in your household growing up? Which ones were your childhood favorites?

If you could recover any possession you've lost, which one would it be?

If you could have witnessed any biblical event, which one would you select?

If you could bring any former leader from the past back to run our country today, who would it be?

If you could spend one whole day with anyone in history, who would it be?

If you could personally witness any event in history, which one would you choose?

What was our most memorable date before getting married?

What has been our most memorable date since we got married?

M
E
M
O
R
I
E
S

Will the passions and flames in our relationship be as strong when we are 60? . . . 70? What will it take to keep the fires stoked?

Which possession do you feel most sentimental about?

What is the kindest thing anyone ever did for you?

What is the most thoughtful thing anyone ever said to you as a child?

Level Four

ASKING ABOUT FAMILY

What do you think the kids need most from me right now as a dad/mom?

In what ways does television affect our relationship as husband and wife? . . . our relationships with our kids? Do we control it or does it control us? How can you tell?

What do I do that makes you feel the most support in our home as a father/mother?

What values are we passing on to our children? In what ways does our lifestyle reinforce those values or undermine them?

Which of your domestic responsibilities do you feel the most confident about? . . . the least confident about? How can I encourage you more in these areas of difficulty?

How effectively do I confront our kids? What suggestions do you have for me in this area?

(husband to wife) Do I come across more as a loving leader or as a demanding boss in our home? What gives me away?

What are we doing today as parents to help our kids get ready for life on their own?

What is my example teaching our kids about what it means to be a husband and father? . . . what it means to be a wife and mother?

How do you feel about the strategy/approach we use for disciplining our children? What steps could we take to improve it? Do you feel my support in this area?

F
A
M
I
L
Y

Am I spending enough time investing myself in the lives of our kids? How can you tell?

Do you feel that my relationship with your family (i.e., your mom and dad) is strong? What steps could I take to make it stronger?

What characteristics do you see in my parents that you hope I'll inherit and pass on to our kids? Which ones do you hope I will not inherit? Why?

What positive and negative characteristics do you already see our children beginning to inherit from us? How does that make you feel?

Are we teaching our kids good manners? How so? What can I do to help you encourage them more?

(husband to wife) Do you feel I do my fair share of the chores around the house? Be honest. Are there ways I could help you more?

How can I more effectively encourage spiritual growth in the lives of our children?

Should we set aside a weekly "Family Together" night— a night to hold a family update meeting, share a devotional time together, and pray as a family? What should it include? How can I help it succeed? Which night of the week?

How do you feel about the order and flow of our home? In what way can I contribute to improving that as a husband and father? . . . as a wife and mother?

F
A
M
I
L
Y

What kinds of things did your mom and dad most often argue about when you were growing up? What have you learned from observing that?

What kinds of unspoken conflicts or tensions existed between your parents when you were in their home? How did those tensions impact you and your home life?

(husband to wife) When do I most remind you of Tim "The Tool Man" Taylor from *Home Improvement?*

In what ways do you think the marriages of our parents affect the marriage you and I share today? Be honest with me.

What are three things a man can do to "build his home"?

What practical steps can I take in my first five minutes at home each night to reconnect with you? . . . with the kids?

When our children grow up and leave our home, what will they say were our strongest values and convictions as a couple?

Do I tend to show favoritism toward any of our kids? In what way? What do you think I could do to correct that tendency?

Do you feel our kids generally respect and honor you as their father/mother? How could I better encourage that trait within them?

What talents/gifts/abilities do you see emerging in each of our kids? What could they become really great at one day? What are we doing to encourage the development of those skills?

F
A
M
I
L
Y

What kind of person do you hope our son/daughter will one day marry? Describe him/her, and be specific. What type of person do you believe will be the best complement and support? Do you know anyone who fits that description?

How did our parents handle the empty-nest experience?

How does the kind of marriage we have affect the kind of parents we are? Explain.

If someone asked our kids today, "How do you know your parents love you?" What would they say?

What tends to come first in our household? What are a few things we always seem to make time for?

Do we maintain a good balance in the various roles you and I fill in life? In other words, do I seem to be able to focus on being a good parent, a good employee, and a good spouse at the same time?

What would we do differently if Jesus were a guest in our home for a week? What would change about our habits, our words, our schedules, our entertainment choices, and our use of time?

(husband to wife) In what way is my treatment of you as my wife teaching our kids about the way a gentleman should treat a lady? Be honest.

In what ways do my actions and words contribute to our children's sense of self-esteem?

Am I communicating the rules and boundaries of our home clearly? . . . consistently?

F
A
M
I
L
Y

As parents do we tend to confront areas of concern in our children appropriately and adequately, or do we tend to put off confrontations?

What are our kids up against spiritually in today's world? What influences do we need to protect them from? How can we most effectively do that?

Psychologist James Dobson says effective discipline of children involves "shaping the will without breaking the spirit." How successful are we at doing that? What improvements could we make?

Do you think I'm patient with our kids most of the time? Tell the truth. What steps do you wish I would take to express more patience toward them? (Hurry up and answer!)

What are some things you think the kids would really love for me to do with them? Any ideas?

Are we training our kids to be decisive? How can you tell? What more could we be doing?

What do we do to make each of our kids feel uniquely significant to us? Do they feel that way?

Does spilt milk from a kid's error usually get a reprimand or a patient response on my part as a dad/mom? Explain.

How does too much TV affect each of our kids? . . . their attitudes? . . . their values (i.e., what's important to them)? . . . their behavior?

Do we do enough as a couple to regulate television viewing in our home? Do we monitor what we, and the kids, watch? Do we effectively limit the amount of viewing hours?

What are five essential values we want our kids to embrace above all others? Which ones do we hope they will one day pass on to their kids?

Are we encouraging creativity in our kids? How so? What more could we do to guide them toward it?

Are we raising our children to be readers? . . . to read books not only because they have to, but also for the joy of reading? When is the last time we took them to the library?

What would happen to our family if we completely turned the television off for one day? . . . for one week? . . . for one month? What effect would it have on our lives? . . . on our relationships? Want to try it?

Are we developing any traditions as a family? Any rituals our kids can look forward to, remember, and one day pass on to their kids? What are they?

Which is more important in our home—rules or relationships? Which one should be the most important? Why?

What are we doing to strengthen our kids' social skills? Are there other steps we could be taking?

What together times as a family can our kids look forward to each week? What are we doing to preserve, protect, and develop those times?

(husband to wife) What chores around the house would you love for the kids and me to help you with?

As our children look back on our marriage one day, what do you hope they will want to emulate?

F
A
M
I
L
Y

Are we helping our children get a good sense of what they want to look for in a potential spouse one day? What can we do to assist them in finding the right mate? How can we do so in a manner that will intrigue rather than frustrate them?

Describe the woman you hope our son will one day marry (or, the man our daughter will marry). Be specific about physical, social, intellectual and spiritual characteristics. Consider this: Does such a person exist? Do you think your expectations are idealistic or realistic?

How could we make our celebration of Christmas (or Easter) more special as a family this year? *(husband to wife)* In what way could I more fully contribute toward that goal as the spiritual leader of our home?

(husband to wife) Does the way I treat our daughter effectively model for her the way we hope boys will one day treat her? What more do you think I could be doing?

What would you and the kids do if a fire broke out in our home during the night? Are we prepared? Do we need to have a fire drill some night?

In what ways do you and I affirm our kids regularly? How could we more effectively and consistently build our children's confidence and sense of self-worth?

If building a home could be described as a recipe, what ingredients do I need to "add to the mix"? What ingredients do you need to add?

F
A
M
I
L
Y

What are our children learning from our example about the relationship between a husband and wife? How do you think our example will one day influence their experience?

What are our children learning from our example about generosity and sharing? How does our example today impact the kind of givers they will be?

How strong are your relationships with the members of your original family? What are the current strengths/weaknesses?

What do you want or need in your relationships with your brothers and sisters?

How can I get the kids to listen to me without yelling at them?

How much work should our children be doing around the house?

What impact is the pace of our lives currently having on our marriage? . . . on our kids?

How do I usually deal with tension "storms" that brew up in our home? Can you suggest a better way for me to do so next time?

Are our children learning to share? How can you tell?

Is our son/daughter learning to accept himself/herself? What can we do to help?

Are we cultivating a materialistic appetite in our children? How can you tell?

What makes a great parent?

F
A
M
I
L
Y

In what ways do we most consistently affirm our children?

Would you like for our kids to be raised in a neighborhood like the one where you grew up? What are your reasons?

Level Five

ASKING ABOUT
FRIENDS AND FRIENDSHIPS

In what ways are our dates now different from what they were before we were married? In what ways are they similar?

In what ways can (or do) I help to relieve stress in your life?

Do we as a couple allow walls of unforgiveness or resentment to build up between us? How quick are we to forgive each other?

How effective am I at confronting you when I have a problem with something? What steps could I take to improve my confrontational style? . . . my timing?

Am I a good listener as a husband/wife? How can you tell?

How proficient am I at being able to tell when you are maxed out with pressures and stresses? Do I usually detect it and respond to those needs within your life and soul?

How do you feel when I fail to keep a promise I've made to you? Does it make a difference if it was large or small?

Do you think of our relationship together as a real friendship? Would you characterize it that way? Why?

Do I most often bring out the best in you? How?

What friends would you like to have over for a visit soon? What can I do to help make it a great night?

What do you think I most need from you as your husband/wife?

How transparent do you think I am with you? What makes you feel that way?

F
R
I
E
N
D
S
&

F
R
I
E
N
D
S
H
I
P
S

Do my words and actions generally build your sense of confidence as a woman, as a wife, as a mother (or as a man, husband, father)? Or do they diminish it? In what way?

Do you know how much I need you in my life? Do you realize the ways in which I need you? Have I told you lately?

How can you tell when people are really listening to you? How can you tell when they're not?

How would you define intimacy? What makes a marriage truly intimate?

How do I generally make you feel when we are around other couples? How could I make you feel more special?

Are there some topics on which we will probably never agree as a couple? Is that all right, or do we need to agree about everything to be really close?

Is there any married couple on television that best represents what you would like our marriage to be like? Why that couple?

Is it fair or productive to use the words "never" or "always" when we're having a disagreement? Explain.

When we have arguments or disagreements, what steps can we take to make sure we stick to the issues and don't drift into personal attacks?

Are there some times when a disagreement needs to be postponed? If so, when? How can we discern those kinds of times?

Just how "together" do the two of us live our lives? What kinds of things would you like to do more of, not independently, but together?

The Bible originally described marriage as a man "leaving his mother and father" and "cleaving to his wife." Do you feel we have done both? Honestly? Thoroughly?

In what ways are we most alike as people?

In what ways are we the most different as people? Do our differences most often collide with or complement one another? Describe.

How would you currently describe our relationship? What adjectives would you use?

If we were to take an inventory on the relational resources within our marriage and home life today, what would you say we are well-stocked with? What are we running short of?

In what general ways are men and women the most different?

When talking with a woman, what is most important for a man to remember?

How do a woman's needs most differ from those of a man?

In what ways do you most need my support? How can I best show or express it?

What are some questions you wish I would ask you more often?

If you could choose, what would be the first thing we said to each other in the morning? . . . the last thing we said to each other at night?

The Bible teaches that we should consider the interests of others before our own (Phil. 2:3-4). In our marriage, do you think I live up to that or fall short of it?

Is our marriage closest to a democracy (a sharing of power), an autocracy (where one person rules), or a theocracy (where God is first and foremost)? What brings you to that conclusion?

Do I most often build your self-esteem or diminish it? In what ways?

The Bible says that "Two are better than one" (Eccl. 4:9). Does our marriage prove that principle to be true? In what ways?

How effective are we at keeping our calendars synchronized? How does it make you feel when you've scheduled an activity that gets bumped because it never made it onto my calendar? How can we improve?

In what ways do you wish I was more like you? Do you think I ever will be?

Over the years, in what ways have we become more like each other?

If there was a book that comprehensively described who you are as a person, how well would you say I have read that book? . . . What chapters have I read thoroughly? Which ones have I only skimmed? Which ones have I completely overlooked? What would the title likely be?

When it comes to the things that build a marriage, what are the best tools you and I have going for us?

Do I tend to interrupt and correct you unnecessarily when you are trying to communicate to someone else? If so, how does that affect you?

If we looked at our marriage as a garden, what are some of the weeds that need to be pulled? What can we do to get rid of them? What can we do to prevent them from coming back?

In what ways have I changed the most since we first got married?

Does our marriage feel like a true partnership? In what way? What contributes the most to that?

Am I usually available and accessible when you really need to talk about something?

How do you feel about the way we resolve conflicts in our relationship? Is it a good method? Is there a pattern to it? Does it work?

In what ways do we both work at making our marriage a great one? What steps are we regularly taking to make it so? How would you say we are doing currently?

Can you tell when I am listening attentively to you? What gives me away?

(husband to wife) Since our wedding day, what have you learned about what it takes to speak "Man"—that is, to communicate in such a way that I really understand you?

(husband to wife) What foremost principle should a man remember when he tries to speak "Woman"—that is, the language women understand?

Do I tend to praise you in front of others? How does that make you feel?

What three women do you respect most? Why?

How openly do I communicate my love for you? . . . for our children?

Which part of the telephone do you tend to use the most—the transmitter or the receiver? What does that tell you about yourself?

What same-sex friendship means the most to you today? Why?

When is the last time we sat down and looked through our wedding photo album together? Want to do that right now?

When it comes to communication, in what ways are men and women the most different? What does it take to overcome those differences?

Am I generally accessible and available when the kids need me? How can you tell?

In what ways do you and I affirm each other regularly? How could we more effectively and consistently build each other's confidence and sense of self-worth?

What people in your life are you the most comfortable with? Why?

How do you feel about our relationships with our neighbors? Would you call them real friendships? Why? Why not?

F
R
I
E
N
D
S
&
F
R
I
E
N
D
S
H
I
P
S

Who is someone you would like to have a better friendship with? What is stopping you?

Do I most often approach marriage as a "giver" or as a "taker"?

Do you feel that I listen deeply to you? How can you tell? What could I do to improve in this area?

Are you an introvert or an extrovert? Does being around people drain you or motivate you?

Which friendships have influenced your life the most? In what way?

Who were your best friends growing up? Tell me about them. What attracted you to them? How did they affect your life at that point?

Level Six

ASKING ABOUT
FEELINGS

What are the three kindest things anyone has ever said to you?

What are the three most painful things anyone has ever said to you?

When do you feel the closest to me?

What do you need from me the most right now as your husband/wife?

How is your "emotional bank" today? Overflowing? Replenished? Almost empty? Overdrawn? Stressed over "bounced checks" (i.e., unkept promises)?

If someone asked you, "How do you know your husband/wife loves you?" what would you say? Be honest.

When do you feel the furthest from me emotionally . . . spiritually?

In what ways has our marriage changed you as a person?

What aspects of married life were the most difficult for you to adjust to?

When do you feel the most beautiful? . . . handsome?

What is the most thoughtful thing you ever remember me doing for you?

Do you feel we have enough time to talk together . . . to share our lives with each other?

What habit of mine do you most wish I would change?

What was your most joyous experience as a child?

F
E
E
L
I
N
G
S

What was your most difficult experience as a child?

The Bible describes marriage as "These two shall become one." How much oneness do you feel we have as a couple? What makes you feel that way?

When do you feel the most lonely?

How do you feel about our schedule—are we too busy or too complacent? What action can we take to reconstruct our calendar so we have time for things that matter most?

In a world so full of unfaithfulness and infidelity, do you ever get fearful or insecure about our relationship? What exactly do you feel? How do you manage those feelings?

In what areas of your life do you feel the most fulfilled? . . . the least fulfilled?

How do you really feel about the way I drive?

What are the three greatest strengths you see in me?

What are the three greatest weaknesses you see in me? Be honest.

What kinds of contact bring you the greatest fulfillment in our relationship? What touches mean the most to you?

At what seasons in our marriage have you felt the greatest distance from me emotionally? What do you think contributed to that?

What causes the greatest stress in your life? What kinds of things contribute the most to it?

(husband to wife) Am I patient and sensitive enough in the sexual side of our relationship?

F
E
E
L
I
N
G
S

What would make me a better lover?

When do you feel the most taken for granted by me? . . . by the kids?

What one trait or characteristic would you most like to change about yourself? Why?

Do you feel you can talk with me about anything—really anything? Or are there some topics you hesitate to broach with me? Why?

Are there needs in your life that you feel I am basically unaware of or insensitive to? What are some of them?

Is a romantic flame still burning in our relationship? What would increase the candlepower?

In what kinds of discussions do I typically become the most quarrelsome or argumentative? Why do you think this happens?

What do you think I expect from you as a marriage partner? Are my expectations realistic or unfair? In what way?

What kinds of situations or topics typically create the most conflict between us? How can we better manage such times as a couple?

When do you feel the most cherished by me?

What are five things that men most often misunderstand about a woman and her needs?

When am I the most romantic? . . . the least romantic?

How open and honest do you feel I am with you?

F
E
E
L
I
N
G
S

Are there any unresolved issues in our relationship that keep us from being closer to one another? If so, what are they?

Which is more important in marriage: avoiding conflict or dealing with the issues despite the conflict it may cause? Explain your feelings and convictions regarding this.

When am I the most difficult to deal with? Be honest.

Do you feel that I genuinely appreciate what you do as a wife and mother? . . . as a husband and father? How can you tell?

What can I do to awaken or enliven the sexual side of you as a man . . . as a woman? In what ways do I most cultivate those desires within you?

When is the best time of the day or night for us to be sexually intimate?

What kind of atmosphere and surroundings are most conducive to sexual intimacy? Describe the ideal setting.

When is our sexual intimacy the most meaningful to you? What makes it that way?

How flexible am I in our marriage? Do you sense I am most often willing or unwilling to bend on the issues we face in managing our home? Over what issues am I the most flexible? . . . the least flexible?

With what feelings are you the most often overcome? Do you know why?

F
E
E
L
I
N
G
S

(husband to wife) In what ways do I tend to overreact as a man and husband? Do you ever feel that approaching some issues with me is like walking into a minefield? Explain your observations.

What are two things I do that regularly upset you?

What does a woman need most from a husband?

What does a man need most from a wife?

According to men, what makes a "good wife"?

(wife to husband) According to you, what makes a "good wife"?

In what ways can I most show that I respect you?

When have you felt most honored by me?

What aspects of being married to me do you find the most challenging? . . . the most exciting?

What is the most draining aspect of motherhood? . . . of fatherhood?

If someone were to ask you, "Is your husband/wife committed to you?" what would you say? If the person continued, "How can you tell?" what would be your response?

Do you ever feel labeled by me in any way? Do you sense that I critically write you off in some aspects of your life or character? How so?

When have you felt the most loved by me?

What am I quick to share with you? What am I slow to share with you?

F
E
E
L
I
N
G
S

When I say that I forgive you, do you usually sense that I have truly freed you from the offense emotionally? Describe.

What is the most fulfilling aspect of motherhood/fatherhood?

Do you feel we have a good marriage? . . . a great marriage? What could make it even better?

(husband to wife) Which do you think is more important to me—your outward appearance or your inner qualities? What makes you feel that way?

Which deceased family member or friend in your life do you tend to find yourself really missing? What about him or her do you miss most?

Do you feel I place boundaries or limitations on your life?

What are they? What do you think causes them? How do they make you feel?

Do you feel excluded from any aspect of my life? How so?

What aspect of my personality or character surprised you the most after we got married? What were you not expecting?

What do I do to encourage your sense of significance and identity as a wife/husband? Anything?

What do I do to encourage your sense of significance and identity as a mother/father? Do I at all?

What do I do to encourage your sense of significance and identity as an individual?

F
E
E
L
I
N
G
S

In what ways are you different as a person when I am around versus when I am not around? Why do you think that is so?

What aspects of my life, schedule, temperament, or habits tend to worry you the most? Why?

What is generally the most frustrating part of your day? Why then?

When is the best time and manner for me to confront you when something is bothering me?

Are there some things you feel we really need to discuss, but I tend to avoid or underestimate their importance? What are they?

What is there too little of in our marriage? Is there too much of anything in it?

What was the most romantic moment we have ever shared together? Describe it. What made it so special?

In what ways does my frame of mind and disposition affect the atmosphere of our home?

Do my words most often build you up or tear you down? Give me an example.

Do I communicate kindness and thoughtfulness to you? In what ways?

Do you know how thankful I am for you? . . . just how much I truly appreciate you? Have I told you recently? . . . specifically?

What has been the most frustrating part of your day today?

F
E
E
L
I
N
G
S

Do you ever feel you don't measure up to some people's expectations in certain areas of your life? How does that make you feel? What do you do to deal with those feelings?

Am I quicker to forgive than when we were first married? If so, how can you tell?

What kinds of things bother you the most? What do you find yourself worrying about?

Do my words and actions regularly affirm you? . . . our children?

What offenses do you find the most difficult to forgive? Why those?

What questions do you wish I would ask you more often? . . . or at all?

Do you ever feel as if you don't have anyone to talk to?

Do I tend to expect too much from you? . . . from the kids? . . . from other people? If so, what effects does that tendency produce?

What aspects of your life and person do I tend to encourage and affirm the most? Which ones do I tend to overlook?

Do I sometimes criticize the things you say before taking time to consider the real feelings behind your words? Tell me about a time when I did that.

What intrigues you the most about me—my accomplishments and performances, or my personality and character? Explain.

F
E
E
L
I
N
G
S

What goals in life do you think motivate me the most? How can you tell?

What experiences do you and I share that tend to renew our closeness and sense of intimacy? In what way? When was the last time we shared together in such a way?

(husband to wife) Do you feel I treat you like a lady when we are among friends or out in public? How so?

(husband to wife) Do you sometimes feel that I expect too much from you as a wife? . . . as a mother? In what ways?

(wife to husband) Do you sometimes feel that I expect too much from you as a husband? . . . as a father? In what ways?

How would you describe the general mood or climate of our household? Overcast? Partly cloudy? Sunny? Warm? Cool? Thundershowers? What factors contribute to that climate?

Would you say I'm attentive to you and your needs at home? . . . when we're around other couples? . . . when we're with my family or your family? How can you tell?

What is the most chaotic part of your day? Why then?

How would you define the word contentment? When do you feel the most content? The least content? What factors contribute the most to your sense of contentment?

What kinds of struggles and situations make you the most angry? Why? What do you generally do with your anger?

F
E
E
L
I
N
G
S

What people in your life are you the least comfortable with? Why? How are you coping in these settings?

(husband to wife) What is it really like to carry an eight-pound human being in your body and give birth? Is there any way you could describe it to me?

Do you regularly get enough sleep? Why or why not? What could I do to help?

Do you feel that we make love often enough?

What fears do you wrestle with the most? How do you manage them?

Do you feel wanted by me? In what way?

With whom do you share your secret sorrows?

With whom do you share your secret joys?

What are the biggest walls you are facing today? . . . we are facing as a couple?

Why do you hesitate to share some things with me?

What do you most regret? How do those feelings impact your life?

What do you enjoy the most about married life? . . . the least?

Do I express my love for you often?

What are the little things I do that bother you the most?

What do you most want/need from our marriage?

F
E
E
L
I
N
G
S

(wife to husband) How do you handle the pressure to provide for our family? What thoughts does that responsibility create, and how does it make you feel?

(wife to husband) Do I add to the pressures you feel to provide for us? How so?

Do you feel you are the most important person in my life? How can you tell?

Are there any activities in my life that you feel are more important to me than you are? If so, what are they?

Are there any special ways I could better communicate how important you are to me?

What is one accomplishment in life you feel proud of?

If your life were suddenly taken today, what would you most regret not having told someone?

Who most inspires you in life? Who do you most admire?

Are you more comfortable around men or women? What accounts for that?

What daily disciplines do you most need to strengthen in your life?

If our house were on fire and all of our loved ones were safely out, what item would you retrieve if you had the chance?

What is the most difficult habit you have ever tried to get rid of?

F
E
E
L
I
N
G
S

How do you usually respond to compliments from me? . . . from others? What causes you to react that way?

Would you consider me a promise keeper? How can you tell?

What touches do you most enjoy in our relationship?

Level Seven

ASKING ABOUT FINANCES

Do you feel we're being good stewards of the money and resources God has given us? What steps could we take to improve?

Do we waste money as a family? In what ways?

What are we teaching our kids about money and how it should be handled? Are we effectively communicating biblical stewardship to them? Does our example bear up to our principles? How could we strengthen those essential areas?

The Bible says, "Where your treasure is, there your heart will be also" (Luke 12:34). If someone took an objective look at where our money goes . . . what would they say is most treasured by us? What if they looked through our checkbook?

If you had to name the dumbest purchase you ever made, what would it be?

If you had to name the wisest purchase you ever made, which would you name?

If you had to donate everything you own to a charity, which one would you choose?

Will there ever be a day when we don't have a car payment? What will it take for us to get there?

What were your mom's and dad's spending habits when you were growing up? Which have you adopted?

Do I add financial pressure to you? In what way?

Are we living on a budget? What would it take to get us onto one?

When is the last time we prayed together about our financial needs and stewardship? Let's pray now!

F
I
N
A
N
C
E
S

How will our financial needs change in the next year? . . . the next five/10/20 years?

How much monthly income will we need to live on when we retire? What steps are we taking today to get ready?

If our income increased next year by $10,000, what would we do with the extra money?

How much money do we need to save for our children's education? What are we doing today to get ready for that expense?

What steps are we taking to ensure that our children have a solid work ethic? Are they catching the idea? How can you tell?

What would we do if our income suddenly decreased by $10,000 annually? Where would we cut our expenses?

Do we make more than we spend or spend more than we make? How much, on average, per month?

Is there ever a good reason to go into debt?

What impact does debt have on the joy we share in our married relationship?

Have ATMs (automated teller machines) been a help to our financial management or a hindrance? In what way?

If we had to cut back our spending considerably in one particular area, which would you choose? What would it require of me? . . . of you?

What are the benefits of delayed gratification? Do we practice that discipline regularly?

F
I
N
A
N
C
E
S

Level Eight

ASKING ABOUT
FAILURES AND FEARS

Which struggles or weaknesses in your life bring you the greatest frustration? Why?

What do you believe were your mother's/father's greatest disappointments in life? How did those disappointments affect them? . . . their marriage? . . . their relationship to you?

Do you feel I'm willing to be vulnerable with you? Do you hear me discussing my struggles and weaknesses with you forthrightly? Describe.

How does it make you feel when I'm willing to share honestly with you about the difficulties in my life?

If my temper fuse could be measured in inches, how long would you say it is?

Do I demonstrate an immediate willingness to deal with difficulties in our marriage? How so?

When it comes to things that tear a marriage apart, in what ways are we closest to the danger zone?

Have you been able to forgive your mother and father for their failures and imperfections that affected you?

What aspects of your life are you most satisfied with today? Which aspects are you least satisfied with? Why?

What mistakes of our parents are you most afraid we will repeat? What do you think it will take to prevent that from happening?

What are our children learning from our example about managing conflicts in life? How do conflicts impact us? How do they tend to impact our kids?

When you're discouraged or disillusioned, how do I usually react?

FAILURES & FEARS

Was there ever a bully in your life? What was he/she like?

Are you generally willing to accept help? Will you ask for it?

What has been the greatest disappointment of your life? How does it affect your life today?

What consuming fears have you most struggled with in life? Who do you tell about them?

Do you think I take myself too seriously or not seriously enough? How can you tell?

What one thing in life right now makes you feel the most hopeless?

When you get knocked down by circumstances in life, do you most often tend to get right back into the boxing ring, or throw in the towel?

Have your greatest lessons in life been learned in the valleys or on the mountaintops?

What impact does fear have on your ability to dream, discover, and dare to try new things in life?

Does our relationship assist you in overcoming fears in your life? In what way?

Can you freely talk to me about your failures? Why or why not?

If you could erase fears in your life, which one would you erase first?

F
A
I
L
U
R
E
S
&
F
E
A
R
S

Level Nine

ASKING ABOUT
THE FUTURE

When you think of the next 10 years, what are you most excited about? What are you most afraid of?

If something ever happened to me and you had to lead this home on your own, what responsibilities are you the most confident you could handle? What responsibilities are you least confident about?

After the kids have left and the nest is empty, what would you like to do more of together? How can we prepare ourselves now for that time?

What house improvements would you most like to see made?

What goals would we like to accomplish in our marriage over the next year? . . . five years? . . . 10 years? Can we discuss them together?

If you could do anything you wanted for the kingdom of God and be guaranteed it would succeed, what would you do?

What are some dreams you have for your life? Do they feel attainable or unattainable at this point? How can I as a spouse better encourage your pursuit of them?

What goals are we going to aim for in the lives of each of our children over the next year? . . . five years? . . . 10 years? . . . 15 years? Can we write some of these down right now and keep a journal or log?

How do you think you will handle the grieving process when your parents pass away? What do you anticipate you will need from me to get through that time?

How will our lives change during the first year of the empty-nest season of life?

THE FUTURE

What will our kids need most from us five years from now? . . . 10 years from now? . . . 20 years from now?

What kind of older woman/man do you want to be one day?

What impact do you think our consistent and loving discipline of our children will have on them 20 years from now?

If you ever had the chance to start a business on your own, perhaps even out of our home, what would it be? What would you call it? How would you start it? How much time would you want to invest in it? How would that affect our lives?

What kind of mother-in-law and father-in-law do you hope we will one day be? What will that goal require of us?

What kind of grandparents do you hope we will be one day? What will it take to get us ready for that task?

What is one thing you wish we had more time for in our lives?

Where is one place you have always wanted to go that we've never visited?

What would you most like to accomplish before you die?

What sport or hobby would you like to take up?

Would you like to paint or sculpt?

Would you like to write a book someday? If so, what would it be about?

Would you like to do some acting one day?

What kind of funeral do you envision for yourself?

T
H
E

F
U
T
U
R
E

Level Ten

ASKING ABOUT FAITH

Could an objective observer of our relationship tell we are a Christian couple? What would give us away?

What do you most need from me to encourage your growth as a Christian?

Would you hold me accountable for screening the media influences that fill our home? In other words, when you see me putting something in front of my eyes that isn't good, will you address it? I need your help.

What makes a married relationship distinctively Christian? How is a Christian couple different from a non-Christian one?

With so many marriages falling apart around us today, what steps can you and I take to ensure that we stay close as a couple, emotionally and spiritually?

How does it make you feel when we pray together? When we haven't prayed together?

Has our faith in God strengthened our marriage relationship? In what ways?

Are we as committed to our church as you would like to be? In what way?

What practical steps can we take as a couple to "affair-proof" our marriage?

What place does prayer have in our home? How could it become more of a priority? What do you think it would require from me?

(husband to wife) When do you most feel my positive influence as a spiritual leader in our home? In our marriage?

F
A
I
T
H

Would you describe your church life as fulfilling? Explain.

What "spiritual gifts" (abilities and talents) do you believe God has given you? In what ways are you able to express them currently? How can I encourage those gifts more fully in your life?

How well do you think I know and understand your soul—the inner person that represents who you are at your deepest level? How can I get to know that part of you better?

How important is the Bible to our marriage, our parenting, and our family? In what practical ways do we bring the Bible into our lives at home? In what ways could we emphasize it more?

In what practical ways does our faith in God make our marriage and our home life stronger?

Back in the 1700s, Jonathan Edwards said a home should function like a "little church." Does ours? In what way?

Since God created marriage, what are some things you believe He has planned for it that most couples tend to miss or overlook?

Are our temperaments as well-prepared for church on Sunday mornings as our clothes are? How can I help make getting our family ready on Sundays more positive for you?

Do the struggles of life ever cause your faith to waver? Do you ever find yourself doubting God, His existence, or His hand upon your life? How do you deal with those feelings and thoughts?

F
A
I
T
H

How does your relationship with God affect your relationship with me? How does your relationship with me impact your relationship with God?

Are we "getting church into our family" as often as we are getting our family into church? In other words, how much is our weekend church life impacting the way we live during the week? Explain.

What steps can we take to encourage our children to maintain a strong sense of moral purity and to preserve their virginity until the day they marry?

Is there any way in which we parent our children that reminds you of the way God "parents" us? How so?

What Bible verses do you find yourself turning to most often when you're facing difficulties in life? In what practical ways do they help you?

When in our married lives have you felt the closest to God? Why then?

When did God become more than just a name to you?

Are we praying together often enough? How can you tell?

What impact would consistent prayer together have on our marriage?

Do you feel at peace with God?

Does your faith help you focus your life? In what way?

What do you think God expects from you?

How does your faith affect your values in life?

How does my faith affect our family? . . . our marriage?

F
A
I
T
H

Is there ever a good reason for missing church?

What would it take to make family prayer and devotions a success in our home?

Can our children sense the love of God through our example? In what way?

Are our kids learning to read their Bibles? What can we do to encourage more of that?

What place do we give to prayer in our home? What is our example teaching our children about its importance?

What does it mean for a couple to be truly "one"?

Surefire Ways to Get to Know Your Kids

Unfortunately, parents are the last people in the world most young people talk to. But it doesn't have to be that way! ***Now We're Talking! Questions That Bring You Closer to Your Kids,*** by Robert C. Crosby, will help you open up lines of communication to build a relationship with each of your children. It's packed with hundreds of specific ways to ask any child—toddler or teen—just about anything. And with its tips on how and when to pose these questions, moms and dads will be happily surprised when their kids, who used to respond only when spoken to, actually begin *talking* with them.